Fingerpower® Fun

Level Three

Compiled, edited and arranged by Wesley Schaum

FOREWORD

The purpose of these pieces is to provide musical experiences beyond the traditional Fingerpower® books. The series offers students fun-to-play melodies which have many technic benefits. The pieces are arranged in order of progressive difficulty and nicely supplement all method books at this level.

A planned variety key signatures, time signatures, syncopations, dynamics, phrase groups and use of staccato helps develop basic musicianship. Any of the pieces would be ideal for recital or school performance.

A short technic preparatory drill ("Finger Workout") focuses on some of the melodic patterns found in each piece (except on page 21).

INDEX

Schaum Publications, Inc.

EXCLUSIVELY DISTRIBUTED BY
HAL•LEONARD®
CORPORATION
7777 W. BLUEMOUND RD. P.O. BOX 13819 MILWAUKEE, WI 53213

ISBN-13: 978-1-936098-70-5

Finger Workout: Play this exercise five times daily as a warm-up for "Runaround."

Runaround

David Biel

Finger Workout: Play this exercise five times daily as a warm-up for "All the Rage."

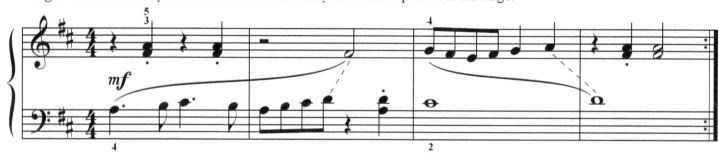

All the Rage

Adapted from
Lavoy Miller Leach

Finger Workout: Play this exercise five times daily as a warm-up for "Basically Blues."

Basically Blues

Andante ♩ = 72-80 *(swing 8ths)*

David Biel

Finger Workout: Play this exercise five times daily as a warm-up for "Really Neato."

Really Neato

Moderato ♩ = 112-120

Wesley Schaum

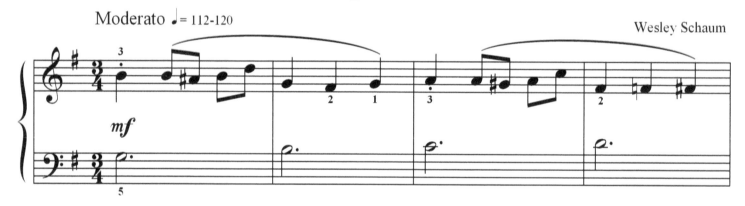

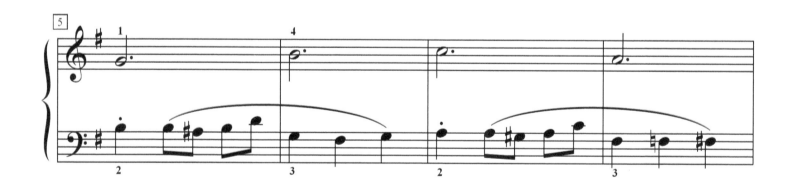

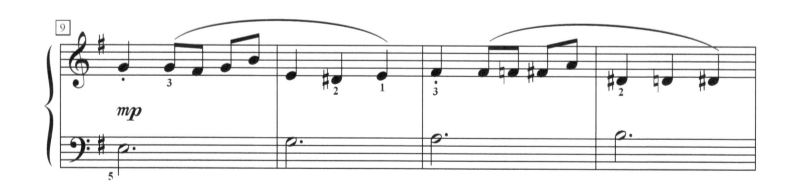

Finger Workout: Play this exercise five times daily as a warm-up for "Barnyard Swinger."

Barnyard Swinger

Con vivo ♩ = 138-152

Kevin Costley

Finger Workout: Play this exercise five times daily as a warm-up for "Easy Does It."

Easy Does It

Andante ♩ = 80-88

Alfred Cahn

Finger Workout: Play this exercise five times daily as a warm-up for "Laid Back Rag."

Laid Back Rag

Giocoso ♩ = 126-138

Stanford King

Finger Workout: Play this exercise five times daily as a warm-up for "Rickety Rock."

Rickety Rock

Stanford King

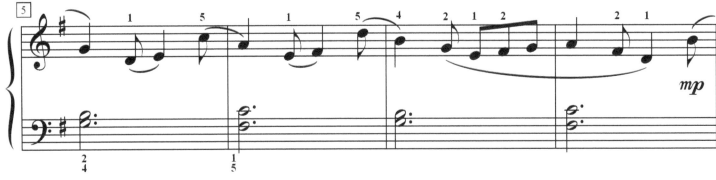

Finger Workout: Play this exercise five times daily as a warm-up for "Fingers Chasing Fingers."

Fingers Chasing Fingers

Vivace ♩ = 116-128

Frank Levin

20

Hey Chattanooga!